WHO MOVED MY OFFICE?

A User's Guide to Life During and <u>After</u> "Lockdown"

By Helmuth G. Cote

Who Moved My Office
© 2020 by Cote, H
All Rights Reserved.

ISBN: 9798644359141

No part of this book may be reproduced in any form or by any electronic or mechanical means including information storage and retrieval systems, without permission in writing from the author and copyright holder(s). The only exception is by a reviewer, who may quote short excerpts in a review.

Cover designed by H. Cote.

This book is a change management business tool. Parts of this text include anecdotes to illustrate concepts and points. Although actual incidents and events may be cited within this text, names, titles and places have been changed or obscured. The focus is intended to be on the content and concepts used as illustrations, not the individual participants.
Any resemblance to actual persons, living or dead, events, or locales is entirely coincidental.

by
Helmuth G. Cote

Please visit our website at www.CoteConsultingServices.com

Printed in the United States of America

First Printing: April 2020

Contents

Who Moved My Office? i
Introduction 2
Embrace the reality 5
Establish Your Beachhead 10
Build a Powerful Routine 16
The Devil Wears Prada 23
Recognize The Opportunities 26
Final Thoughts 32
Next Steps & Acknowledgements 34

Dedication

This book, and my entire life, is dedicated to my amazing wife, Jamie Cote. Without her love, guidance, patience and support neither this book nor anything else I do in life would have a fraction of the meaning it now holds.

Jamie is not only my partner in life, but also my partner in business. As you progress through this book, you will encounter passages about health, workout regimen, nutrition, meal planning, diet and routine. Make no mistake. My personal examples are not entirely of my own design. They were largely designed by my wife who cares enough to do the research and wants me to succeed in all things in life, not the least of which is staying healthy in body and mind. She keeps me young in more ways than one.

Her constant support during late nights and odd hours as I wrote this book (and others), worked on websites, written songs and screenplays, developed material and succumbed to my workaholic tendencies has been unwavering. She was always there providing me <u>exactly</u> what I needed when I needed it whether that be a hot cup of tea, a meal, a hug, space to create or suggesting I seek balance in my efforts. I am grateful to have a true partner in life that stands by my side through it all and supports my passions and goals with a hefty dose of reality, all without squashing my dreams.

For that, I am eternally grateful and wouldn't have it any other way.

About the Author

* * *

As a business system software implementation consultant and project manager, I have worked from a remote (home) office for the lion's share of the last 27+ years (as of the writing of this book). A U.S. Navy veteran with nearly 20 years of leadership experience, I have an innate ability to adapt to a rapidly changing environment to lead my team to emerge victoriously.

I have been a member of a remote team, following and leading, building skills and experience to successfully collaborate with team mates, clients, subordinates and management. When not on the road, I perform my duties from my home office. When on the road, I get my work done wherever I can, transforming literally any space into an ad-hoc office. It might be an airplane seat, airport chair (or barstool), a hotel room, a hotel lobby, a customer's conference room, table at a restaurant or sitting in my rental car.

I have worked in traditional office settings in both corporate and government/public service and understand the pitfalls, challenges, frustrations and opportunities inherent with navigating a transition from corporate space to remote space.

Today I am a published author, published singer/song-writer, business systems consultant, project manager, nutritional coach, executive coach, digital leadership expert and soon to be the host of the Good News Blues podcast where I merge two of my passions: blues music and spreading positivity. I hold a Bachelor of Arts Degree (Summa Cum Laude) in Business/E-Business from the University of Phoenix.

I have learned the formula to success in working remotely and leading remote teams and experienced the pitfalls that lead to failure. It is my sincere hope that you can find yourself in the lessons I teach which are grounded in the hard lessons I have learned. It is my desire for you to my teachings as tools to emerge more confident, productive, and unapologetic in your pursuit of success.

I currently live near Chicago, IL with my beautiful, ambitious, talented and generous wife Jamie and our dog Scarlett. They are both at once a constant example of the importance of approaching each new day with passion, enthusiasm and gratitude; and, the best distractions a man could have from the curve balls life throws. They keep me grounded and provide valuable perspective. And make me smile.

One of my all-time favorite quotes is from my wife, "We don't deserve dogs." I echo that sentiment in that I don't deserve my wife, but I am certainly better for the gift of her presence in my life and I am extremely grateful for it.

Forward
By
Jamie Cote

A new normal has been defined during this crisis. This new normal will continue beyond the pandemic of 2020, and working from home will just be normal. Learning to navigate the strange unfamiliar waters will be critical in not only surviving but also in striving past 2020.

I learned to work from during the few relocations my husband was offered in his career. I am Jamie Cote. Yes that last name is the author's name, and I am his wife.

We have forged the unknown of spouses working from home while moving, planning a wedding, and dealing with massive medical issues. And Helmuth was the rock and authority on making it work.

He has taught me everything I know about working from home, and over the past 10 years have applied to fully transitioning to working from home, now self-employed. He has decades of experience working remotely, from cars, planes, hotels, and more. And his discipline from his military career provides even more bulk to his knowledge of being successful.

This book is the saving grace that you will need to manage yourself, your home and your new normal office locale during the current crisis survival mode and long after.

Jamie Cote
April 11, 2020
St. Charles, IL

INTRODUCTION

Pivot. I can't personally recall hearing that word used very much. That is, not until lately. But as I started writing this during the last two weeks of March 2020 with the pandemic in full upswing and the world is reacting to it in full panic mode, it's being said more often than Ross Geller telling Rachel and Chandler how to help him get his new sofa up the stairs!

Pivot! Pivot!! Piv-OT!!!

But somehow today – it's not as funny. It's not a fictional sofa being pushed, prodded and pulled up a narrow winding staircase by some fictional characters on a television sitcom. It is the essence of our once stable careers and lives tumbling down a very real staircase and potentially trampling us along the way.

The future is fraught with uncertainty and unease. Unease in the stock market. Unease in if we or our loved ones will catch the virus, and if so, will we survive? Unease in what this will mean to our lives, our livelihood, our jobs and the world economy at large. There is in the midst of all of this, one certainty:
Change.

Years ago, I sat on a commercial flight from Chicago to some city or another, en route another consulting gig. Just before take-off, a complete stranger finished reading a small paperback book. I saw him close the book, then ponder for a moment while a smile slowly spread across his face. I didn't avert my eyes in time, so he caught me looking. Busted!

The next thing he did changed my life. He handed me the book and said, "Read this. You need it even if you don't know it yet. We all do."

The book was "Who Moved My Cheese?" by Spencer Johnson. If you haven't read it, you need to. Right after you finish reading this book.

I took it, thanked him and started reading. By the time I looked up from it, I had finished the book and we were on final approach to wherever we were going. I tried to return it to its rightful owner. But he refused and said, "Pass it on." And with that he was gone in a bustling crowd that was racing off the plane to find their own Cheese.

In a nutshell, that book is about four mythical creatures who go off to explore a fictional maze every day in search of metaphorical "cheese." Ultimately, they all find their cheese, but one day they show up and the cheese is gone! Two of the mythical creatures were already noticing the supply was dwindling and were preparing to find new cheese. The other two were blindsided by the fact their precious cheese was gone and as a result, they were paralyzed. Instead of focusing on finding more cheese, the obsessed on the fact that somebody moved their cheese.

The reader comes to realize the lesson of the parable is far less to do with the missing cheese or, as the title suggest "who moved" it. It has far more to do with mind-set and learning to ask better questions. Face it, at the end of the day, does it matter who moved your cheese? No! The cheese is gone. Maybe you should have seen it disappearing, maybe you shouldn't have – but none of that matters. It is gone. The immediate question you should be asking is "How do I find more cheese?" And then you need to get to work and put yourself in a position where it never happens again.

So, as we face this certain uncertainty in our lives, we can either choose to sit idly by and watch our precious sofa crash to the floor, likely taking us with it...while we're wrapped around the axle trying to figure out whose fault it is; or, we can choose to adapt and respond in a way that will not only ensure that we survive, but that we thrive! (And maybe save the sofa and keep the cheese multiplying in the process.)

This book is about asking the better question. Once you accept that it doesn't matter who (or even why) your office has moved, how will you execute an action plan to respond. Trust me: You will not only feel better, you will be better as a result.

Like its predecessor namesake, this is book teaches you how to adapt to change. But more than that, it's also a story about the triumphs available to you when you do adapt with the right mind-set. Unlike the earlier book, I'm going to cut right to the cheese, er, I mean chase.

So let's attack this together, shall we?

EMBRACE THE REALITY

Chapter One

"Sometimes you have to accept the fact that certain things will never go back to how they used to be." - Unknown

Who moved my office? That is the question so many people woke up one day in the first few months of 2020 and started asking as the entire world made a global shift from working in offices to working from home – all in the interest of practicing safe social distancing. Here in America, this shift started happening in earnest around the middle of March. Like a train wreck unfolding in slow-motion, we all sat there watching the world in disbelief unable to look away and unable to comprehend the obvious: This IS happening to me.

I'm here to tell you: that is the wrong question. STOP ASKING IT! I am a firm believer that the answers we get are only as good as the questions we ask. So if you want a better answer, ask a better question. I hear you thinking, "Okay, genius...what would be a better question?" Well, that's not it either. We should all start with an immediate self-assessment.

My career in the U.S. Navy spanned from the tail end of Vietnam through the Cold War and up to the Persian Gulf War (the first one). During that time I operated primarily as a Naval Aircrewman. That meant that a lot of my time was spent performing my duties aboard multi-place Navy aircraft. That's just another way of saying a plane that carries more than one person. Sometimes these were land-based aircraft, sometimes they were carrier-based. In order to be qualified for such duty, I had to undergo some very harsh, specialized survival training. At the very heart of it was learning how to survive in the event of a bailout, an aircraft crash or ditching (controlled crash at sea). I used this training later in my career when I personally crashed into the reality of civilian life when my Navy career suddenly and unexpectedly came to an abrupt, screeching halt. That directly applies to the situation we all find ourselves in now and I would be remiss not to share my knowledge and experiences with you.

The first thing we were taught was the importance of taking inventory after the dust settles. Basically, that means asking yourself, "Am I okay?" You want to determine if you are bleeding and make sure that you have all your arms, legs, fingers, toes. Actually COUNT them, because in the state of shock you might not notice your arm is no longer there. If you find out that you are bleeding, then you have to take immediate action to stop the bleeding so you can get on with the task of surviving. As soon as you know if you are okay, or have stabilized yourself if you are not, you ask the next question, "Is my crew okay?" Do you see the difference? These questions drive action instead of fester worry and anxiety.

You take the same inventory you did on yourself, but now focusing on your team. First, determine if you know where they all are and if they are alive or injured. You communicate with them and gather them together. You assess how badly they are suffering from the shock and if they can be of assistance to you and rest of the crew. You let them know that they are not alone! (in doing so, you are reminding yourself that *you* are not alone.) Once that task is accomplished you ask one more "discovery" question before doing anything else. You ask, "What do we have that will help us survive until we are rescued."

Let's break down that last question because the psychology of it is crucial. There are three critical elements in that question that are the foundation of maintaining a positive mind-set in a post-disaster scenario. A positive mind-set and mental attitude is absolutely essential to survival. It gives you the ability to lead, even if you are the lowest person on the totem pole. It doesn't matter if we are talking about a crash of an airplane, a loss of your job, a relationship imploding or a crash of the world economy. It all translates.

What do we have...? You must have an honest assessment of any resources at your disposal that add value to your situation. It is so common to overlook something valuable because it isn't obvious that it could help you. The obvious things are the survival equipment and supplies that you made sure were on the plane or on your person before take-off: Food, water, medical/first aid kit, survival knife, emergency radio, etc. Once you make sure that you still have those things, and know where they are, you start looking for other assets. Do I have access to my parachute? Are there pieces of the airplane available to me? If I crashed on land, where are the survival rafts? (if you crashed at sea, hopefully you are *in* the raft.) Those things can all be used as shelter to protect you and your crew from the sun or rain.

What do I have **that will help us survive**...? This is important because it puts you in the positive mind set that you are looking for ways to survive. That survival is the only option. As long as you are seeking a way to survive, you are in a much better place with more chances of success than sitting around grousing about why you are in this situation and how long it's going to be before you die. Does it matter? Can you do anything about it? No! So don't waste your time feeling sorry for yourself. Sorrow and negativity are the enemy. You must defeat them. And the way you can do that is by remaining positive and becoming proactive. Adopt this mental shift and your crew will immediately identify you as a leader. More than anything, they need a leader right now. They are going to follow your example regardless, so why not give them a positive role model?

What do we have that will help us survive **until we are rescued**? This might be the most important element of that question. It speaks to hope. Have you heard the saying Name it & Claim it? This is so vital to survival and putting you on the road to success. It is actually a break-through. Face it. You just crashed in a freaking airplane. You have two choices – let the situation define you (read: sit around waiting to die) or define the situation to the outcome you want *and deserve*.

By now I'm sure I may be losing some of you. Don't leave. I know you're probably saying to yourself, "I wasn't in the Navy or in a plane crash so how can this possibly apply to me?" It applies directly to you and the position you woke up and found yourself in. It doesn't matter if your office has been relocated or you got fired or laid-off. It doesn't matter if it happened last week, last decade or ten years from now. You need to take the same basic steps I've outlined above to put yourself in the right mental attitude to not only survive, but thrive. You must accept the reality of what is happening, but do it in a positive mindset. This bears repeating: <u>Feeling sorry for yourself won't help you or anyone else</u>. Own this new reality. It is yours. Embrace it. It might be the only hug you get today.

APPLICATION:

Take a moment right now and reflect. Are you okay? Count your fingers & toes! Take inventory spiritually, emotionally, and financially. What about your team. Your family, your colleagues, your friends. If not, what are you able to do RIGHT NOW to stop the bleeding? Get creative! Now go do it. This book will be here when you get back.

If you are okay (or okay enough to continue for the moment), what assets do you have that will help you survive until you are rescued? Open your eyes, look around you & be creative. You may be surprised at the assets you take for granted. Recognizing them will give you two gifts: security and gratitude. Unwrap the gifts.

ESTABLISH YOUR BEACHHEAD

Chapter Two

"The plan is useless, but planning is essential."
- Dwight D. Eisenhower

You used to have a "home base" at your office. For many of you, your corporate office environment was a place where you felt safe. It was your powerbase. You felt in control. You knew your shit and the person sitting beside you or down the hall from you respected you for it. If you allow yourself to admit it, you might have derived more worth from your "at work" self than you do from your at-home self. And now your clearly defined ying & yang has been plopped in a blender and somebody hit the puree button. So now what?

The good news is, you still have that same powerbase, regardless of where your office is physically located. Your change in real estate is the least of your problems. Now you have to cultivate a change in mind-set to keep from losing your sense of value, confidence and worth. And let's be honest. Do not approach this new "normal" as temporary. For many of us, that is not the case at all. I am a firm believer the Corona Virus Pandemic of 2020 is forcing a new reality on us all. And that reality is that the world is experiencing an era of fundamentally changing the way we do business and live our lives. When the "lockdown" is over, fewer of you will be returning to a commercial real estate brick and mortar corporate office space. And even if you do, the lessons taught in this book will position you as a more valuable, more confident and more productive employee.

So one of the first things you need to do in order to be successful is to establish your new beachhead. For those of you unfamiliar with this term it is of military origin. A beachhead is defined by the Oxford English dictionary as: "a defended position on a beach taken from the enemy by landing forces, from which an attack can be launched." This is kind of fitting especially if you do not already have a designated home office. In strict military terms, a beachhead is a temporary line created when a military unit reaches a landing beach by sea and begins to defend the area while other reinforcements help out until a unit large enough to begin advancing has arrived. But there are two important things to remember here. Temporary in this case doesn't necessarily mean you will be returning to the relative safety of your landing ship (read: corporate office tower). And, most importantly, YOU might be your own reinforcements. Let's break that down.

You are establishing a temporary workspace until you hit your groove, so-to-speak. Once you find your rhythm, get your mojo, however you want to phrase it, your new temporary office may well become your permanent office. But initially there are going to be stressors here that you never even thought of and even with the help of this book, you are not going to master managing them overnight. A beachhead remains a beachhead while you learn the environment and the enemy and establish supply lines. Then that beachhead might become a established command post or even a headquarters. Right now, you are tactical in every sense of the word, so establish your beachhead.

Build yourself a safe place from which you can launch attacks. An area of power. You need to make a space where you can work, talk, think, be creative and be productive. A place where you can successfully attack each new day and all the ups and downs that will unfold along the way. It doesn't have to be exactly like you had (have?) in your office building, but it must be conducive to making you feel like you can effectively conduct business. If you don't have a perfect home office, that's okay. Now is the time to be creative.

The obvious things you are going to need will be the basics that you can put into place immediately and build from it. I'm going to assume that you have internet access at your home (if you don't have it, you will need it). You will need a computer or tablet that not only connects to your home internet, but also has all the tools that you will need to access any resources that are currently at your place of business or on the cloud. This may include network share drives, printers (in case there is anyone in the office and you need to print something directly for them), etc. This usually requires some type of virtual private network (VPN) client on your laptop/table that gives you a secure connection to your corporate network. I will assume that your company IT department has already been enlisted to provide this. <u>Be nice to them</u>. They are a key ally at the moment and you depend on them for your success. Make a note right now to put them on your Christmas (or Kwanza or whatever) card mailing list.

So what else do you need? Great question! When considering your office space, take into account background in the event you will be on video conferences. That means that whatever is behind you will be seen by others on the meeting. So choose a location that is both well-lit and doesn't have a lot of foot traffic passing behind you. Also consider if there are any highly personal art, books, etc. in the background. During meetings you will want participants focusing on you, not your background. This also applies to background noise which can be very distracting to everyone when you are trying be taken seriously and making that career breakthrough presentation.

The space needs to be as quiet and as isolated as possible. This is for many reasons. First and foremost, let's assume you will be needing to conduct phone conversations. You will need a quiet place for this, and face it, a ton of American families are two income households. This means that there may well be <u>at least</u> two of you vying for prime home office real estate. Everyone deserves enough privacy to conduct their business without adversely affecting their new "co-worker(s) down the hall."

But you also have to be realistic. This maybe the first time in, well – ever, that you and your spouse/significant other have had to be under the same roof 24x7 for an extended period of time, competing for "corporate" and domestic resources. As much as you (both?) need as professional of a work environment as possible, there may be other distractions such as children who need home schooling (or a hug) or pets that may require your attention. When they gotta go they gotta go, right? Plan for it. Either be ready, willing and able to offer up an explanation why you need to step away from a video or telephone conference, or make preparations to have someone cover those moments for you. Make no mistake – these interruptions <u>will</u> happen. The good news is, the people on the other end of the line are experiencing the same thing. This isn't permission to be unprofessional, this is permission to be real, authentic and transparent!

Set ground rules and expectations with your family turned new co-workers. Open lines of communication are vital to not only your work success, but more importantly, your home relationship(s) success. If you have an established schedule based on set meeting times on specific days (which I *HIGHLY* recommend), it is so much easier for your spouse/significant other, adult child, father-in-law, etc. to work around them – not only for their work schedule but also for the home routine in general. This will help everyone be more effective at work while getting along better at home.

Set office hours and stick to them. Do not be tempted by the thought that your desk is just right over there as an excuse to keep working beyond your normal hours. You will burn out and you will alienate your family. And it sets unrealistic expectations with your actual co-workers and manager(s) when to expect you to be productive and when not to. It's okay to have boundaries. In fact, it is essential.

In summary, once you've established your physical power base, you have established your beachhead, which is nothing more than a place from which to launch your assault on the challenges that each day will bring. Make sure it is a place where you feel as safe, powerful and confident as you can. But also remember to be realistic about being flexible. Certainly have a plan, but accept that the plan is probably going to have to be thrown out and rebuilt as you go. At first it will feel like you've jumped out of an airplane and now you are trying to figure out how to put on your parachute while hurling toward the ground at 122 mph. It's okay. You'll get used to it. You may even learn to like it. Trust me.

APPLICATION:

Take a moment and reflect. Now might be the perfect time to call a family meeting and establish your beachhead. Make a checklist of everything that you _need_ "not want" to successfully work from home. To the extent possible, re-purpose what you have. Remember, we are about to enter into a nasty recession. Cash is king and don't spend on anything you don't have to. Talk to friends and relatives if there is office furniture that you need and don't have. They may have something to lend you or give you if they are getting rid of it. If you must buy, look for bargains. You don't need new. Write down your schedule, to the extent you can, and post it where everybody in the household can see it. Remind each other to remain flexible and supportive of each other as you navigate this together.

TIP: Don't forget to have fun! In fact, stop what you are doing right now and smile. Force it if you have to. Remember what they say, "Fake it 'till you make it!" There are tons of activities you can do on your own or as a family. Recreation is key to keeping from burning out. Look at the very word: re + creation. It's the way you can re-create energy, zest, perspective and relationships. Don't overlook this gift.

BUILD A POWERFUL ROUTINE

Chapter Three

"Winning is a habit. Unfortunately, so is losing."
– Vince Lombardi

Routine is one of the most important parts of your success strategy. It's what puts you in the right mindset from the moment you wake up until the moment you fall asleep. What you do becomes a habit, so why not develop positive habits? As we learned earlier, a positive mindset is essential to surviving in the face of adverse conditions whether they be a plane crash or having your work life (and life in general) turned upside down. A routine keeps you focused and centered. It also keeps you focusing on the tasks at hand so you are not drawn into the temptation of being paralyzed by the fear and uncertainty of living in the future. We can all use a lot more of that especially right now. Go ahead and *plan* for the future, but *live* in today.

I cannot stress enough how important it is to enlist your spouse/significant other, and all family members, in supporting your routine. And you must support theirs. Everybody has to be onboard. That does not mean that everybody has to have the same routine.

This is the routine my wife and I have built for me while she has her own routine that meets her daily needs and demands. It certainly doesn't have to be yours, but I offer it as an example of what works for me.

Each day my alarm goes off early. Before leaving bed, I make sure to kiss my wife, tell her I love her and that I am grateful for her. Most mornings she stirs or wakes, other mornings she does not. I have an agenda. It's important to me for her to not feel alone when she wakes up. It is a little thing we do for each other and part of our over-arching communication routine – which if I'm honest, she is way better at than I. Then I spend about a minute in prayer telling my Creator how grateful I am.

Next I repeat a mantra in my head that I recently learned, telling myself that I am happier, healthier, wealthier and more fit today than I was yesterday. I actually do this several times per day. I find it helps me at once be grateful and remain focused on whatever I am working to achieve that day. Eyes on the prize, so to speak. It is so much easier to produce from a place of gratitude and abundance than from a place of scarcity, negativity and feeling over-whelmed. So I mainlining positivity. I recommend that you do, too.. You don't have to do this exactly as I do, but find something that works for you. Something that gets you excited about getting out of bed. Something that sets yourself up to feel successful before your feet even hit the floor. You will be amazed at how your day will unfold and how much you will accomplish, compared to waking up cursing your alarm, complaining about being up so %&$# early and thinking about all the negative mental clutter that you might have taken to bed subconsciously. So get yourself right in your head.

Next I dress in my workout clothes and, along with our beautiful black lab Scarlett, we head down to our modest home gym in the basement. I stop at the bottom of the basement stairs and turn on the coffee pot. Next I turn on all the lights to help wake myself up, then cross the basement to in front of the television and put out Scarlett's blanket that she likes to lay on while I get my work out in. I return to the coffee pot and brew one cup that I will consume during my 10 minutes of allowed news input to get updated with what happened over night while I stretch. Ten minutes. Period. I even set an alarm. Why? Because I know that if I let myself, I will sit in front of the television and let the negative propaganda soak into my brain robbing me of my work out and my positive outlook. I know I am capable of going down the rabbit hole, so I protect against it. If I don't get my work out, I don't get my endorphins. If I don't get my endorphins and let the negativity in the world impact me, my cortisol levels rise. Then I start feeling, looking and acting sluggish and the body fat starts to increase. And it's just vicious downhill cycle from there. More like an avalanche than a snowball effect. So for the sake of my own mental health, it's 10 minutes of news. Period. And then work out. My morning workout is my mental floss.

I feel like I should make another important note here about routine building and communication. As I said before, not everybody in the house needs to be on the same routine for everything throughout the day. It is helpful if the main schedule points are aligned, like dinner time and maybe even bed time. But certain things will be according to your own individual schedules and bio-rhythms – and that's ok. You have to do what makes sense for you. In our home, working out is one of those things. It's important to both my wife and I, but choose different times in the day to do our workout. By doing this, we achieve the best work out possible. Since it is a home gym, it is rather modest and somewhat limited in equipment. Competition for resources would be an issue if we were both working out at the same time. And face it, sometimes you just need "you" time. I need mine and she needs hers. It is healthy to recognize that and plan for it. Not to mention, my work day starts before hers, so she doesn't have to be up as early and I get to take the dog out on the early morning run as gift to her. That's not to say we don't do things together. Often while she is working out, especially on weekends, I will grab my laptop and write in the basement while she works out. Some mornings we all go for a walk together.

I should also mention that if I somehow skip a step in my morning routine, our little Scarlett sits in front of where I'm supposed to be until I get back on track. She only needs once in a row to build a habit. I'm told people need 21 days in a row. I probably need way more.

During my workout, I am intentional about feeding my mind & soul while exercising my body. So I decide whether I'm going to listen to a uplifting podcast or music. I decide and turn it on. Currently, I am following a workout on an app that my beautiful wife found. I pull it up on my phone, hit play and start my work out with my podcast or music flowing in the background.

I set another alarm to signify my workout is over. That does two things. Relieves me from clock watching so I can focus on what I'm there to do. And it prevents me from cutting into other structured sections of my day by going too long in the gym (it could happen). I know I personally need boundaries, so I use the tools I have to create that structure. Don't be afraid to use your tools to create structure.

Scarlett and I clean up the basement and head upstairs to leave for our morning walk/run/trot around the neighbor. It takes us a few minutes to get out of the door, and our target is to be back just in time for her breakfast (6:30 AM). Then it's shower time, dress for work and start my day by 7 am. Notice I said "dress for work." I will cover this in detail in in the next chapter.

Diet and nutrition play a huge part of my daily routine. During a normal day, my wife and I have our breakfast together which is a nutrient-enriched meal replacement protein shake. Sometime mid-morning we take a break and have our morning snack together and around noon we have our lunch together, another protein shake. Our afternoon snack time is typically independent of one another, usually dictated by my schedule for client calls and webinars. Then it's time for dinner. She cooks (because I like to eat good food) and I clean up. It's a partnership. Diet really deserves a chapter unto itself, actually an entire book. But I'm not the one to do it. I listen to my wife. She is currently serving our various communities by offering resources for meal plans, meal prep guidelines, healthy eating tips & tricks all aimed at teaching you how to boost your immune system while staying on a tight budget.

This is another slippery slope area especially during the current shelter-in-place "lock down." Right now especially, I would bet a ton of people are emotional eating. Couple that with not getting out of the house and getting the exercise you need and possibly being sleep deprived due to stress and worry – and you have yourself a perfect storm on your hands that will impact you physically and mentally. And not in a good way. You've heard it said before, "You are what you eat." If you eat like crap, you're going to feel like crap. And if you feel like crap, just how well are you going to be performing from that new beachhead you just built? For more insight on my tools for diet and nutrition, follow my nutritional coach - Jamie Cote on Facebook and @the_jamie_cote on

Instagram and be one of the first to get her new cookbook she is about to release!

Finally, I end each day in prayer with my wife. We typically do this right after we get in bed. We focus on thanks and gratitude and ask for insight into ways we can serve others and fulfill ourselves. That puts us in the right frame of mind to wake up positive and repeat.

Of course some (non-quarantine) days I travel. If it's a flight day, it's an entirely different routine. If I'm on the road, it's the same routine but without Jamie & Scarlett. Regardless, it is a routine. And it's important to me. And I protect it at all costs. That is really the take away here. Be a boss – and bosses don't cancel on themselves.

Harkening back to my naval aviation survival training, routine is a critical element of what to do in event of a bailout or plane crash. Build a routine. Give your crew something to do. If everyone is focused on doing something to improve their situation, they don't have time to get caught up in the fear of the unknown. Lead by example - you owe this to them.

If you would typically stop for coffee on the way to your office, swing by your new favorite "drive-through" (i.e. your kitchen...) and pour yourself a cup of coffee on your "commute." If you normally work out before work, by all means continue to work out now. Don't succumb to the temptation to get an extra half-hour sleep because all you have to do is walk downstairs to go to work. Instead, find something positive to do during that found time to pour love into yourself. Find something that fills you up and add it to your routine. I cannot over emphasize the importance of having a powerful routine.

I'll leave you with a final thought on creating your office and establishing your beachhead. I quote Jodi Picoult, an American writer with over 14 million copies of her work in print, "If you focus on sandbagging the beachhead, you can ignore the tsunami that's approaching. Try it any other way and you'll go crazy."

My Daily Routine:
4:30 AM   ALARM
4:35 AM   In Gym. Pre-work out coffee & 10 minutes of news update while stretching
5:30 AM   Wrap up work out, ready for run
6:30 AM   Feed the dog, take a shower, dress for work
7:00 AM   Begin work day
10:30 AM Morning snack
12:00 PM Lunch with wife, together take walk with dog
12:45 PM Back to work.
3:00 PM   Afternoon Snack
6:00 PM   Wrap up work for the day. Assist with dinner, feed dog
7:00–10:00 PM Work on any unfinished business, watch TV with wife & play with dog
10:00 PM Set gym clothes out for tomorrow. Bedtime. Prayer & sleep.

APPLICATION:

Take a moment and reflect. Do you already have a routine or do you need to build a new one? Sometimes it just takes a little tweak to an existing routine to make it fit the "new normal." Is your family onboard with your routine? Do they even know your routine? Do you know their's?

What are you going to do, starting TODAY, to implement a powerful routine? If you have printed this off, use the space below to jot down your commitments. Or get paper & pen or type it. However you want to document it, document it. Then share it with somebody that will help hold you accountable. Sometimes social media accountability posts are the best for that! Go ahead and write it down. Do it now right now:

Your Daily Routine:

THE DEVIL WEARS PRADA

Chapter Four

"The way we dress, affects the way we think, the way we feel, the way we act and the way others react to us."
– Judith Rasband

Its also been said that the devil is in the details. Bear with me and we will see how these two connect. Now that you've established your beachhead, you've set ground rules, you've told your boss when to expect you to be on the phones, returning e-mails, etc. Maybe you have put your schedule on a white board on your home office wall so everybody can see it (hint, hint). Your dog knows when you will take her on a walk, you spouse knows when to count on you for dinner, their time with you, etc., etc., etc.

You're feeling confident and powerful. You and your team are a bit shaken up, but everybody is okay and you've accepted the reality that you will survive, even if the search party doesn't find you.

Actually, you might be surprised at just how good you're feeling right now. Stay realistic. Stay positive. Get productive.

So you throw on your sweat pants and comfy t-shirt to head to the office, right? WRONG! That is not unless you would have worn your sweat pants and comfy t-shirt to your cubicle or office before our sudden WFH (work-from-home) shift.

What you wear has an enormous effect on how successful you are. And it's not just about how others view you, it's far more important about how you view yourself. Again, it speaks to that all important mind-set. In a study done by The Journal of Experimental Phycology and published in the Wall Street Journal results showed that in a role-play of negotiating the sale of a high-value asset, better dressed negotiators achieved a better result. How much better? Great question! Well-dressed negotiators realized a profit of more than $2M vs poorly dressed negotiators who only achieved an average of $680,000. Well- dressed negotiators conceded an average of $830,000 vs poorly dressed negotiators who conceded nearly $3M. I don't know about you, but I want a piece of that pie! I deserve it! So I will dress for it. It is important to note, this role-play was regardless of whether the negotiation took place in person, via video conference, over the phone or via e-mail. In other words, it didn't matter how others saw you as much as it mattered how you saw yourself.

Okay, now let's apply this to your situation. Dressing professionally means that you have more self-respect, more confidence and more drive. If your boss sees you on a video conference, it means you have his or her confidence that you are taking your work seriously. If they see you in sweats and a t-shirt, they might have the impression that you're not being all you can be, inviting more scrutiny on how well you are doing your job. Who needs that? Not you, right?

So to recap, don't wear it working from home if you wouldn't show up at corporate wearing it. If you have ambitions of climbing the corporate ladder, then remember the mantra, "Don't dress for the job you have, dress for the job you want." Yes – *even* when working from home. Now let's get to work.

APPLICATION:

Take a moment and reflect. No literally, this time. Look at your reflection in the mirror. Be objective. If you were your boss (or your subordinate for that matter), what would you think about what you are wearing right now? Is it "work appropriate?" If not, what would you change? If you are working while you are reading this and there is something you would change about your appearance, stop what you are doing and go change it.

(Hint: You might even consider soliciting (and following) the advice of your new "co-workers.")

RECOGNIZE THE OPPORTUNITIES

Chapter Five

"In confusion there is profit"
—Lt. Watson (quoting Lt(jg) Nicholas Holden in
<u>Operation Petticoat</u> *© 1959 Universal*

This chapter, to be fair, is more geared toward those who have become intentional or accidental entrepreneurs out of all of during this time. However, it applies to everyone whether you lost your job and need to replace your income or if you are wanting to make sure you are never in this situation again unsure of your financial future and are looking for ways to invent new income. Maybe you want to pay down debt, stick it to the man, or thumb your nose at the family members who ever doubted your success due to their own inadequacies. It really doesn't matter why.

At any given time any of us may want, or need, to reinvent ourselves. There is nothing wrong with that. I believe it is incredibly healthy.

I was exposed to the concept of looking for opportunities at a very young age. It is a page out of Sun Tzu's play book who said, "In chaos there is opportunity." History has proven this time and time again. Look at the businesses that came out of the Great Recession in 2008-2010. Venmo, Groupon, Instagram, Uber. None of these businesses existed before 2008. Someone saw a need and recognized they had skills and experience to offer a solution, so a (successful) business was born.

Speaking of the Great Recession, let's talk about the Great Depression. This was a period that spanned from August 1929 through March of 1933. Many used to blame the 1929 historic stock market crash of 1929 as the cause of the Great Depression. Actually, the reverse is the opposite. The stock market crashed as a result of entering into the depression, the subsequent loss of consumer confidence, coupled with a very weak banking system. But that is another topic for another day or a book written by another guy. Suffice it to say it was an economically painful 43 months. Unfortunately, it's probably more on par with what we are about to go through in 2020-2021 than the 2008-2010 Great Recession. But I digress. Instead, I'm about to regale you (or bore you) with some personal Cote family history.

In the 1920's my paternal grandfather was an upholsterer in the automotive industry. He worked for Chrysler beginning in 1925. He was not just an upholsterer, he was a Master Upholsterer and worked on the interiors of the upscale automobiles of the time. When the Great Depression hit, he was finally let go. But he didn't quit or give up. He made a pivot. He had built a beautiful brick home in Southfield, Michigan with his bare hands where he ended up raising a family of eight children. While he built the home, the family lived in a U.S. Army surplus tent from WWI. Detached from the home was a brick garage, with a cement driveway leading from the dirt road. He built the home and the garage before the Great Depression and long before he had a car. Let that sink in.

After he was laid off from Chrysler, he made an offer on some of their commercial sewing machines and upholstery equipment. Knowing the company was in dire straits, he bought them for pennies on the dollar and immediately setup shop in his garage doing – you guessed it: auto upholstery. The way he figured it, there were two things working in his favor. 1) The uber wealthy (not Uber, they didn't exist back then), and the government, still had a need for automobiles and Chrysler no longer had the ability to craft the custom interiors; and, 2) People who already had automobiles were going to try to make them last as long as possible instead of replacing them. Even wealthy people. So he became a contract supplier to Chrysler (and others) and in no time at all, had a line of new Chrysler (and other company automobiles) lined up around the block waiting for his services. He thrived during the Great Depression and when the music started back up, Chrysler extended a generous offer for him to come back to work at the plant. He politely declined and issued them a hefty price increase in return. Well played, Grandpa, well played.

My dad was a WWII Navy vet (Frogman) and had a penchant for campy WWII Navy films. Looking back, I'm 100% certain he was using humor to cope with PTSD (before PTSD was even a thing). Every time *Operation Petticoat* or *Mr. Roberts* aired on network television we gathered as a family around a large bowl of freshly popped popcorn and watched, waiting for dad's gut busting belly laugh and him parroting his favorite lines. "In confusion there is profit" was probably his all-time favorite and he would quote it often, then follow with a story about his dad and the pivot he made during the Great Depression. Dad usually punctuated his stories about grandpa with colorful similes that I will omit here, in the interest of keeping this text uncensored.

Remember I said "network television." This was way before cable and smack in the middle of the age of rabbit ear antennas for the average Joe or roof top antennas owned by those whom we viewed as uber wealthy. This meant dad would assign someone to stand "antenna watch," a duty that required the assigned swabbie to occasionally move around the antenna to make sure the broadcasted signal was received as clearly as possible. As the lowest ranking sailor in the family unit, I usually got drafted. To a young five-year old boy it was super confusing. Move the antenna to the left! (My left or your left?) Stop when the picture is clear. (Seriously? I'm standing behind the TV, how can I see how clear the picture is?) Listen for it! (Listen for the picture? This isn't making much sense.) Meanwhile, my brother and sister divided the bowl of popcorn in half, instead of equal thirds. To her credit, my sister always tried to save me some of her half, but even at five years old it didn't take me long to learn that half (or less) of half, isn't as good as a third of the whole. So in my confusion was their profit. Talk about irony. It was a valuable lesson for which I am grateful today, but it certainly didn't seem like it in the moment. (Side note: to this day I subconsciously hoard the popcorn bucket and I still LOVE both of those movies.)

So what does this have to do with Who Moved My Office? Again – your office was moved. Hell, maybe it up and disappeared. That's a historical fact at this point, a non-negotiable. So the better question is, "What value I can bring to others who might be experiencing this feeling for the first time in their life."

And let's face it. I've said it before, this isn't a temporary thing. This may very well be a permanent shift in doing business for the foreseeable future. If employees can be productive from home why would they want to put themselves through the expense, stress and dangers of a daily commute? If remote teams can be productive, why would organizations want the overhead & expense of a commercial real estate foot print just so someone had a desk, a break room and a coffee pot to call "home?" The answer to both is obvious – they would not. It's a classic example of why fix what ain't broke! This pandemic, for all its horribleness, may have fixed an aging paradigm that no longer serves society the way it once did. In much the same way that it didn't break our world economy, it was just the straw that took the camel to its knees.

APPLICATION:

Examine your skill set. Examine your life. Are you in the midst of this chaos? What skill and expertise do you have that could serve others? This doesn't have to be a career change. Maybe it will help you be more valuable to your organization and will result in a promotion. Maybe it will be a career change. It's been said that the economic crises around this horrible illness will create more bankruptcies, more divorces, more suicides than medical deaths resulting from the pandemic. The good news is that right now, if you are experiencing a pivotal shift, then I urge you to look for a logical pivot.

Every time I start to feel myself get overwhelmed and fearful or anxious about the new state of the world, I force myself to say this little mantra that came to me about two weeks ago. According to Amazon, I'm not allowed to mention the actual official name of these viral infection, but that's okay. I'm using it as an acronym that represents what I've learned out of this #AloneTogether pandemic experience:

Creating **O**pportunities (through) **V**ision, **I**ngenuity & **D**emand.

It's another way of saying, "Never Give Up." Perhaps this picture says it better than my words:

FINAL THOUGHTS

Chapter Six

"If you can't summarize an issue on one page, you don't understand the issue well enough." – Ronald Reagan

In summary, here are the key points to successfully navigate your new reality. Maybe you are working from home. Maybe you are not working at all. Using the concepts presented here will help you not only survive, but thrive.

We discussed how important it is to ask the right questions to dictate your success. Don't ask a question like who moved my office, unless that is really the answer you want. Instead ask a question that incites actions and drives results that move you closer to your goal – whatever that goal might be.

Next we investigated real-world application of what it means to work from home. And how tempting it is to treat it like something else. You are still doing a job and you still have the same expectations of productivity, so why not approach it with as much vigor and professionalism (if not more) than you would if you were driving to an office outside of your home each day. And by the way, be grateful for the curtailed commute. Use that time to better yourself and become more valuable.

Positive mind-set: It is imperative to maintain professional grooming standards – even if nobody sees you. In the world of voice broadcasting, professionals will tell you that if you want people to hear you smile, then actually smile. It comes right through the microphone. The same applies to appearing professional to your audience, regardless if they are actually seeing you.

Finally, I wrote about the importance of always looking for opportunity. For millions of years the human brain has evolved to avoid the dinosaur that is trying to eat us and in the interest of survival, if we don't know what something is, we err on the safe side and assume it's a dinosaur trying to eat us. But we have to retrain our brain and instead of look for opportunity. For example, if the dinosaur gets close enough, I can kill it and feed the village. This shift in thinking allows us to act from a relaxed place of power instead of react from a fearful place of feeling overwhelmed. It takes hard work and discipline, but you can train yourself to seek opportunity. And when you do, you will notice opportunity everywhere.

NEXT STEPS & ACKNOWLEDGEMENTS

Epilogue

"Don't dwell on what went wrong. Instead, focus on what to do next. Spend your energies on moving forward toward finding an answer." – Denis Waitley

Wow! What a powerful quote. If I could only do that consistently. That is my daily goal and some days I do better than others. So where do you go from here? That is a good question. A better question is, "What do I want next, and what am I able to do to achieve it?" I'm just really happy that you're asking questions. You will learn to perfect them if you ask them enough. Good job!

It really is that simple. If you are ready to take the next step in self-realization and if you have found my teachings in this book to be of value, then I humbly ask you to do two things. Please leave me a 5-star review and share this with someone whom you think would benefit from it. Then check out my online courses on digital teams & digital leadership coming mid-April 2020. You can find my course offerings at CoteConsultingServices.com. Check out the website for additional limited time offers during this trying time. We are all in this together.

If you are interested in how to eat healthy while boosting your immune system without breaking the bank, Follow Jamie Cote on Facebook, @jamieLcote on Instagram & subscribe to her healthy cooking/meal prep videos on YouTube (The Jamie Cote). Watch for some exciting launches from her coming soon!

If you are tired of getting bombarded with negative propaganda and are looking for some recommendations on positive propaganda check out one of my favorite podcasts, "For The Love of Money" by Chris W. Harder. Don't miss his powerful story.

Finally, if you want to just veg out for a little bit, check out my military fiction action-thriller *American Infidel* available as both paperback and Kindle e-book on Amazon.com. Search for *American Infidel* by Helmuth G. Cote or find me on my Facebook author's page: Helmuth G. Cote.

If you are ready to up-level your game, visit our website and click on Resources link to view all of our products.

www.coteconsultingservices.com/services

I strongly recommend that you enrol in one of our online e-courses: "*Working In The Cloud: Unmasking The Mysteries of Working From Home*" Or "*Leading From The Cloud: Unmasking The Mysteries of Leading Remote Teams*" especially designed for those serving in a management or leadership role.

May God richly bless and reward your efforts. Thank you!

www.ingramcontent.com/pod-product-compliance
Lightning Source LLC
Chambersburg PA
CBHW050305220526
45465CB00002B/835